YOUR KNOWLEDGE HAS VALUE

- We will publish your bachelor's and
  master's thesis, essays and papers

- Your own eBook and book -
  sold worldwide in all relevant shops

- Earn money with each sale

Upload your text at www.GRIN.com
and publish for free

GRIN

Bibliographic information published by the German National Library:

The German National Library lists this publication in the National Bibliography; detailed bibliographic data are available on the Internet at http://dnb.dnb.de .

This book is copyright material and must not be copied, reproduced, transferred, distributed, leased, licensed or publicly performed or used in any way except as specifically permitted in writing by the publishers, as allowed under the terms and conditions under which it was purchased or as strictly permitted by applicable copyright law. Any unauthorized distribution or use of this text may be a direct infringement of the author s and publisher s rights and those responsible may be liable in law accordingly.

Imprint:

Copyright © 2015 GRIN Verlag, Open Publishing GmbH
Print and binding: Books on Demand GmbH, Norderstedt Germany
ISBN: 978-3-668-05084-6

This book at GRIN:

http://www.grin.com/en/e-book/306836/entrepreneurial-cognitive-factors-and-new-product-innovation-in-37-countries

Charlène Mao

Entrepreneurial cognitive factors and new product innovation in 37 countries. The moderating effects of Hofstede's cultural dimensions

GRIN Publishing

GRIN - Your knowledge has value

Since its foundation in 1998, GRIN has specialized in publishing academic texts by students, college teachers and other academics as e-book and printed book. The website www.grin.com is an ideal platform for presenting term papers, final papers, scientific essays, dissertations and specialist books.

Visit us on the internet:

http://www.grin.com/

http://www.facebook.com/grincom

http://www.twitter.com/grin_com

A literature review from a dissertation submitted to
Tongji University in conformity with the requirements for
the degree of Master of Management

Entrepreneurial cognitive factors and new product innovation in 37 countries: the moderating effects of Hofstede's cultural dimensions

Candidate: MAO Charlène

School/Department: School of Economics and Management

Discipline: Management

Major: Enterprise Management

July 2015

Table of contents

Literature Review

During the previous years, numerous studies have been published around the world in order to determine the factors that could influence entrepreneurs in their new product development process. This literature review will first evaluate all the concepts linked to the principal concept of entrepreneurship. Then the cognitive factors, which could influence entrepreneurship, will be analyzed in details, and finally the environmental effects on entrepreneurial new product development will be investigated.

1. The Concept of Entrepreneurship

Entrepreneurship is considered as "the successful creation and capture of economic rents in the face of uncertainty and scarcity; it enables talented individuals to realize rewards that exceed the equilibrium level of perfect competition and so to live better than others as gauged in subjective utility terms" (Montanye, 2006, p.567). Innovating process identifies itself and takes into account more and more business opportunities in order to create innovative new venture in an ambiguous environment (Amit, Glosten & Muller, 1993). Entrepreneurship can be approached by different ways such as by traits, demographic, cognitive or according to the environment (Chuanyin, 2014). For example, among those entrepreneurial traits, there are different qualities, which should be considered, such as the risk-taking susceptibility, the internal locus of control, the need for achievement, and the tolerance for ambiguity. Nevertheless, reality is not as simple, entrepreneurs do not fit into only one distinctive group, and both personal characteristics and the environment are to be considered.

According to professor Schumpeter (1939), innovation is nearly at the center of all the economical phenomena of the capitalist society. It is also defined as "an idea, practice, or object that is perceived as new by an individual or other unit of adoption" (Rogers, 1995, p.11). It is a co-creation process that focuses solely on the value added perceived by the consumer. Therefore, it is imperative that a sustainable competitive advantage is found through the process of a new product development (O'Regan, 2012). Actually, one of the most important key driven factors for entrepreneurs is to propose innovative products or inventive services in their new venture creation. Some of the entrepreneurs can be considered as inventors; as they have new ideas and concepts that they use in order to create new business. Those people have a high level of self-efficacy; and their main ability is to convert their thoughts and understandings into entrepreneurial activities (Markman, Balkin and Baron, 2002).

Entrepreneurs are people who have actually managed to establish and found their own business because they are confident enough, they believe in themselves, and more especially they believe in their abilities (Chen, Greene, & Crick, 1998). Sánchez, Carballo and Gutiérrez (2011) defined the entrepreneur as a mere business owner who is also an opportunity hunter and is constantly seeking for business growth. They innovate by finding new business models and they manage to raise financial resources in order to sustain their firm creation or development. Moreover, they are also characterized by cognitive attributes such as being risk takers, self-efficacy persons, decision makers able to set up business goals, innovative environment creators, cultivators of investor relations, and they are able to cope with unforeseen challenges. Inside an organization, entrepreneurs need teams and groups as being a pool of people, who can later contribute to the firm policy and its original vision by having unique skills and resources (Contiu, Gabor, & Stefanescu, 2012).

According to Miller (2015), entrepreneurs are self-confident, they take initiatives under risky and uncertain conditions, they are not afraid of facing challenges and they are perseverant even though they may suffer from failures. Furthermore, they are innovators who are constantly renewing themselves and their concepts even after the success. Therefore, they are self-confident, they are looking for more accomplishments and they have the need to control and dominate in their new venture. Nevertheless, some of them can be aggressive, authoritarian and impatient, especially in the founder-patriarch business type. Therefore, entrepreneurs tend to be described as "Janus-faced" because they have both positive and negative attributes.

On a psychological level, people who can control their emotions are more likely to believe in themselves and thus they are thought to be able to succeed in entrepreneurial activities. Emotional intelligence is then an important part in the process of becoming successful in entrepreneurship. It can also be improved and mastered through training in order to increase self-confidence and to encourage innovation by creating value and by having entrepreneurial behaviors (Mortan & al, 2014).

2. Cognitive factors influencing entrepreneurial new product development

A high rate of entrepreneurship will mechanically increases the probabilities that knowledge be transformed into new-to-the market innovation. Consequently, some authors said that knowledge is commercialized into innovative novel products (Block, Thurik & Zhou, 2013). The phenomenon of entrepreneurship, upstream of the new product development process, is influenced by a great variety of factors at different levels of action. In the present part, only the different cognitive aspects will be studied and analyzed. Lately, more and more studies and publications whose main topic is linked to the cognitive approach of entrepreneurship have been published. They mainly describe entrepreneurial behavior and entrepreneurs themselves.

2.1. Self-efficacy

Self-efficacy is itself an important individual determinant of entrepreneurship, as it can explain human behavior because of its impacts on people's choices, efforts and perseverance (Chen, Gully & Eden, 2004). Entrepreneurs are individuals with a high level of self-efficacy, as they will continuously keep on persevering until their initial goals are actually considered as being achieved. In the long run, they tend to set up somewhat higher personal objectives. Actually, the rate of self-efficacy is linked to the persistence and the past successful experiences of the entrepreneur, as those two factors can effectively influence and increase one's sense of self-efficacy. Furthermore, incremental beliefs are thought to enhance entrepreneurial abilities and business success as well as achievements (Gist, 1989).

Training can also be determinant for aspiring entrepreneurs as it can help them to have a better understanding of themselves and their past actions. Entrepreneurial activities are regulated by self-reflection and self-regulation, which when both combined can help to increase self-efficacy (Arora, Haynie & Laurence, 2013). In addition, a high self-efficacy rate is primordial and crucial to some entrepreneurial activities like the creation of start-ups. Believing in oneself will of course bolster one's self-confidence, which is an essential characteristic in entrepreneurship (Cassar & Friedman, 2009). Nonetheless, an excessive rate of self-efficacy can lead to disastrous results, as it will be a source of overconfidence, which will cause negative impacts on various aspects such as decision making process and other skills (Koellinge, Minniti & Schade, 2006).

Self-efficacy, goal specificity and firm creation process are closely linked. Self-efficacy influences entrepreneurs' motivation, which will determine whether or not they can grasp opportunities (Hechavarria, Renko & Matthews, 2012).

2.2. Risk perception

Risk perception is always associated with entrepreneurship, and one interesting fact about this crucial quality is that it differs according to the gender among entrepreneurs. Women's risk-taking self-efficacy is lower than men's in fields such as financial risks or business development; this phenomenon can be explained by the difference of perception and the sense of comparison between one's own task performances and the task performances of others. Hence, women will need more feedback about the quality of the results obtained by their decisions and choices (Forlani, 2013).

Fourati & Affes (2014) have found out that the entrepreneurs belong to three types of risk taker. They can encounter different sorts of risks during the process of a new firm creation. First, high-risk taking entrepreneurs consider the personal and financial risks as a threat because they actually finance their business thanks to external investments. They can be considered as being low-risk taking entrepreneurs if they perceive the risk not a threat, but a missing opportunity they should have grasped. Risk taking entrepreneurs are those who deliberately choose to limit the quantity of their personal funding. Therefore, according to the source of funds, entrepreneurs will not take the same degree of risks. Nonetheless, entrepreneurs who will use external financial investments tend to reduce their chance to grow their business as they rely on an already identified opportunity (Bhidé, 1992).

According to Gartner and Liao (2012), relying on risk perception alone cannot make a clear distinction and classification for the profile of the entrepreneurs. Furthermore, risk perception also seems not to be a determinant factor to predict the success of new venture creation. Among the population, people who have a higher tendency to take strategic or non-strategic risk can either be entrepreneurs or non-entrepreneurs. As the previous studies show, there is not any statistical difference between these two groups about risk propensity (Xu & Reuf, 2004).

3. Individual aspects of the entrepreneurial new product development

Entrepreneurial new product development is influenced and controlled by various internal factors such as individual traits. In this part, only the age, the gender and the education of entrepreneurs will be analyzed.

3.1. Age

The age distribution of population is deeply correlated to entrepreneurial activities carried out by this population. For instance, a high number of young people in certain population will have a positive effect on nascent entrepreneurship, while on the contrary an older population will have negative impact on business creation. As entrepreneurship is essential for the economic development, it can be clear that areas with an aging population will have to face economic difficulties. Aging countries will then have to create public policies in order to attract young entrepreneurs from overseas, and they will also have to support and promote senior entrepreneurs, more especially to help them to have an access to financial investments (Lamotte & Colovic, 2013).

Nevertheless, senior entrepreneurs cannot only be seen as a burden of the economic landscape. By having a significant range of experience and by having cultivated a wide professional network, older entrepreneurs are also crucial for the economic life of a country. They can cooperate with younger entrepreneurs who will directly benefit from them. They can ask their elders for advice to help them succeed in their business. Entrepreneurs under 30 years old will generally seek advice from people within their closest circle, i.e. their families or friends. Those between 30 and 39 years old will more likely to seek advice from the business world, which is to say for instance professional consultants. New business owners who are 40 years old or more usually state that they do not need advice as they would rely on their own personal experience (Robinson & Stubberud, 2014).

Besides, older potential entrepreneurs are way more likely to think of becoming self-employed compared to younger potential entrepreneurs. However, they will hardly choose owner-managed business or to self-employ due to an absence of job opportunities. Consequently, it can be clearly noticed that the age has a certain influence on entrepreneurial activities (Kautonen, Down & Minniti, 2014).

3.2. Gender

According to Wilson, Kickul and Marlino (2007), entrepreneurship might be perceived as part of an especially male-dominated activity, and this harmful stereotype can prevent a lot of unconfident women with low self-efficacy skills to opt for an entrepreneur related career. A lack of confidence from women can easily change their career decisions. According to their perception of their own self-efficacy, they tend to avoid some entrepreneurial jobs even though they already have the necessary skills required by such a job (Bussey & Bandura, 1999). Nevertheless, this problem can be dealt with by introducing entrepreneurial education courses at the earliest stages in order to decrease the biased image that women have of entrepreneurship, to promote a healthier and more gender equal vision of the business world. Such courses can help to boost self-efficacy amongst aspiring women entrepreneurs and help them to acquire valuable entrepreneurship skills (Wilson & al., 2009).

There is also a particular relationship between gender-role orientation and self-efficacy, which can influence entrepreneurial tasks. Some of them require "male" qualities whereas others would need more "female" qualities. It all depends on the process phase in which those entrepreneurial tasks will take place (Mueller & Dato-On, 2008). For instance, for most early stage tasks like searching and planning, these tasks will probably require innovative and creative skills. Those sets of skills can be optimal when they are actually a mix of male and female qualities. However, for later stages it would seem that a more male oriented set of skills would suits better for different tasks, as for instance for persuasion and leading tasks.

Both culture and gender have a significant impact on the entrepreneurial perceived barriers and the entrepreneurial intentions, which can lead to a somewhat hindered way to entrepreneurship for women. The gender difference influence is mostly found in the perception of the environment and also concerning the level of self-motivation. Women are more concerned about this harmful influence than men, and people who perceive those barriers too strongly can be limited to be engaged in entrepreneurial activities. Entrepreneurial education can help to remove the fear of failure and increase the self-efficacy and confidence among aspiring female entrepreneurs (Shinnar, Giacomin, & Janssen, 2012).

3.3. Education

Working culture is closely linked to a society and to the times and actuality it is going through, thus there is a development of entrepreneurial skills along the development of technologies and new discoveries. Studdard, Dawson and Jackson (2013) had proposed the groundbreaking idea to teach entrepreneurship at the primary and secondary levels of education. For example, a K-12 level's program is a success-oriented entrepreneurship education course aimed at children with guest speakers. It will teach them about applying projects and business plan competitions. The authors recommended increasing the number of women and minorities in order to include them and to give them more opportunities to become an entrepreneur, when society usually does not give them such possibilities. Adults can also perceive the process of new firm creation as a career option with the transition from one job to another (Kanter, 1989).

Rozell and al (2010) proposed to introduce new venture training programs in higher spheres of education, which can not only help to develop and promote entrepreneurial skills, but can also have the useful specificity of being adapted to the culture of the targeted country. In transitive economies, entrepreneurship education programs are part of the tools used to incite the students to become more creative and innovative. Consequently, such educational measures will improve their entrepreneurial self-efficacy. The governments also play a decisive role in the promotion of entrepreneurship awareness by connecting the innovators and the graduated business students (Drnovsek & Glas, 2002).

4. Environment effects on entrepreneurial new product development

Entrepreneurial new product development is also profoundly influenced by external factors such as the environment in which the entrepreneurial activities take place. In the present part, different factors will be investigated such as the economic development, the technology level, the export intensity, the public media, the TEA opportunities and eventually the cultural.

4.1. Economic development

New enterprises created by entrepreneurial activities have the potential to foster economic growth or GDP, productivity and innovation (Aghion & al., 2009). According to Noseleit (2013), entrepreneurship is positively related to a direct economic growth and it is one of the many solutions to develop for countries, which are facing necessary structural change. Thus, entrepreneurial activities have different impacts on economic development according to their income (Stel, Carree & Thurik, 2005). Actually, GDP per capita, the average income and the culture have effects on entrepreneurial activities (Liñán & Fernández-Serrano, 2014). Wennekers and al. (2005) have stated that the level of development is closely related to other factors linked to entrepreneurial activities. There is a U-shape relationship between the proportion of start-up firms and the economic development.

Governments usually establish policies on business, international trade, and the mobility of persons or goods. Thus, they have the power necessary to bring a change to the business environment. Thus, they need to create a good environment for business creation; on the one hand, they have to motivate entrepreneurs by imposing different preferential policies that support economic growth due to a rise of employment, and on the other hand they have to build a national culture, which will boost entrepreneurial activities (Lee & Peterson, 2000). For instance, they can launch various public policies to provide financial supports, cut taxes and reduce administrative constraints. Moreover, governance has an indirect consequence on the economic growth; thus it is positively related to entrepreneurship, which as mentioned earlier is also a factor that improves the economic development (Méndez-Picazo, Galindo-Martín, & Ribeiro- Soriano, 2012).

4.2. Technology level

Nowadays, in a fast-changing environment with constantly found new technological discoveries and innovations, the product life cycle has been drastically reduced. The technological uncertainty depends on cultural traits; moreover, some companies make technological alliances in order to develop continuous innovation (Steensma & al., 2000). Therefore, in developing countries the different technology transfers and investments have a positive impact on the targeted country.

Those measures contribute to increase the technology level of those areas. However, they have to be customized and tailored in order to fit the specific cultural and social needs (Kumar & Kelly, 2006).

Technological entrepreneurs have to deal with many challenges in order to transform their ideas into a business model, and later on to commercialize them. For instance they have to handle the risk reduction for investors; they have to recruit skilled employees, they have to ceaselessly update their knowledge, eventually they have to take into account customers' feedback for the creation of new products (Umesh, Jessup & Huynh, 2007). One usual way to protect newly found technologies is to create patents. The patents thus have a positive effect on new venture creation and on economic growth. As a conclusion, it is important to mention that the technology level of a country is deeply related to the actual innovation and the number of patents that are filed within a country (Markatou & Stournaras, 2013).

4.3. Export

Entrepreneurs from diverse countries can establish business relationships through the export market. They need to focus on two processes: the process of planning up export markets and the process of relationship development. Nonetheless, each territory has different cultural values that will influence their own business practices. It is particularly true for the level of trust: Both parties have to accept the difference of relationship imbued by the disparity in the level and the nature of trust (Dibben, Harris & Wheeler, 2003).

The level of intended export is influenced by human and social factors, but not by cognitive factors such as self-efficacy and risk perception. Previous international entrepreneurship experience will also have a positive influence on future international scale business intentions, while domestic new venture experience will have a rather negative influence on it. If a nascent entrepreneur knows someone in his/her network that has already created a business abroad within last two years, his/her level of intention can be increased within the first year of firm's existence (Evald, Klyver & Christensen, 2011).

Export entrepreneurship is not only positively related to various internal factors as export commitment and the different available resources, external factors like the industry level of one's country or its competition, but also by the distance of the targeted market. Export entrepreneurs must pay attention to external markets in order to find new business opportunities. They have to adapt their business structure to the process of internationalization and they have to make an international benchmark with a competitive watch (Navarro-García, 2015).

4.4. Public Media

There is a positive relationship between entrepreneurship heard in the media stories and the entrepreneurship activities of young business in a country. Thus, the mass communication has a compelling role in the society as it can drastically increase entrepreneurship intentions (Hindle & Klyver, 2007). On the one hand, the public media can influence general entrepreneurship; as they can support entrepreneurial practices and attitudes within a country. On the other hand, innovative entrepreneurship, especially those creative and cultural-based businesses, also has a high influence on media industries. The media like to diffuse innovative, creative new way of thinking linked to new business success stories (Hang & Van Weezel, 2005).

Nowadays, entrepreneurs can also rely on their use of social media like Twitter or Facebook as a marketing tool: they can utilize the data in order to improve their social media marketing campaigns. Even if the social media tools are easy to learn and to use, entrepreneurs should not forget that it is highly important that they rely on a solid marketing strategy to build the brand of the company among the potential consumers (Geho & Dangelo, 2012).

4.5. TEA opportunities

Total Early-Stage Activity measures the proportion of working-age adults within a country. They are either nascent entrepreneurs, involved in the process of venture creation, or they can be active adults, like owner-managers of firms less than 42 months. There is a difference between opportunity TEA and necessity TEA. For instance, opportunity TEA means that entrepreneurs are willing to carry out business opportunities, whereas necessity TEA includes only those who do not have other choices, hence the necessity entrepreneurs. However, a high rate of entrepreneurship does not necessarily means that it will lead to any good economic performance and economic growth (Poh Kam, Yuen Ping & Erkko, 2005).

Opportunity is a subjective concept linked to one's perception. An opportunity is basically related to who will perceive it the first and will undertake entrepreneurial activities (McMullen & Shepherd, 2006). Besides, entrepreneurial opportunities are the possibilities encountered to transform already existing ideas into new goods, services, and organizational methods that can be sold with a marge of profit (Shane, 2000). Entrepreneurs benefit from those opportunities to launch their business with product or services. The latter will need to have some added value compared to the already existing products or services.

This statement is confirmed in poverty alleviation environment by Alvarez & Barney (2014), there are different types of entrepreneurial opportunities within poverty context, like self-employment, the discovery of opportunities and the creations of opportunities. Concerning self-employment opportunities in that situation, it is important to note that they are not sustainable solutions.

4.6. Culture

Culture is considered as the most crucial factor influencing entrepreneurship as it is "the most critical set of social and cultural values along with the appropriate social, economic and political institutions that legitimize and encourage the pursuit of entrepreneurial opportunity" (Reynolds, Hay & Camp, 1999, p.43). Liñán, Fernández-Serrano and Romero (2013) have found out that both economic development and culture have a dramatic impact on the pursuit of entrepreneurship. For instance, in developing countries, there is a mix of cultural values and specific policies that promote the raise of incomes as well as the development of entrepreneurial activities. Nevertheless, some regions in the world suffer from a strikingly unbalanced combination of culture and economic development. For example, in Asia, the Southeast part presents a higher level of entrepreneurship than the East and South parts. This phenomenon is explained by the local business policies, which are more sustained than elsewhere in the Asian cultural area. Hence, an open and competitive business environment will have a positive impact on entrepreneurship (Swierczek & Quang, 2004).

The culture influences not only the individual creativity, but also the whole innovation of one's country on a macro-scale level (Williams & McGuire, 2010). Thus, the cultural impacts on entrepreneurial new product development are not to be overlooked. Hopp and Stephan (2012) postulated that there are differences among entrepreneurs according to the scale they were analyzing. They found discrepancies linked to the levels, such as on a sub-national level, on a community level or on a cultural one. They have noticed that performance-based culture tends to enhance entrepreneurial skills such as self-efficacy and enterprise creation motivation. Furthermore, entrepreneurs' motivation can be influenced by social institution supports, which are more likely based on community-level cultural norms. Consequently, culture induces entrepreneurial thinking and behaviors alike.

Entrepreneurial orientation is influenced by the national culture, the culture industry and also by the corporate culture of a certain territory (Fayolle, Basso & Bouchard, 2010). National culture can prove to be a stimulus of entrepreneurial activities as it structures the institutions, which affect the local economic context (Hayton & al., 2002). The culture affects the entrepreneurial networking habits mainly because the entrepreneurs' behavior when developing their social network will be governed and defined according to cultural norms and practices of one's country (Klyver & Foley, 2012). Thus, it depends on whether entrepreneurs belong to a mainstream or a minority culture. Entrepreneurs coming from a minority culture background will have to take into account both cultures at the same time as the demands of the market mechanically tend to correspond to the needs of the mainstream culture.

Bibliography

Amit, R., Glosten, L. & Muller, H. 1993. Challenges to Theory Development in Entrepreneurship Research. *Journal of Management Studies*, 30(5): 815-834.

Aghion, P., Blundell, R., Griffith, R., Howitt, P. & Prantl, S. 2009. The Effects of Entry on Incumbent Innovation and Productivity. *The Review of Economics and Statistics*, 91 (1): 20–32.

Alvarez, S., & Barney, J. 2014. Entrepreneurial Opportunities and Poverty Alleviation. *Entrepreneurship: Theory & Practice*, 38(1):159-184.

Arora, P., Haynie, J., & Laurence, G. 2013. Counterfactual Thinking and Entrepreneurial Self-Efficacy: The Moderating Role of Self-Esteem and Dispositional Affect. *Entrepreneurship: Theory & Practice*, 37(2):359-385.

Bhidé, A. 1992. Bootstrap Finance: The Art of Start-Ups. *Harvard Business Review,* 70(6):109–117.

Block, J., Thurik, R., & Zhou, H. 2013. What turns knowledge into innovative products? The role of entrepreneurship and knowledge spillovers, *Journal Of Evolutionary Economics*, 23(4): 693-718.

Bussey, K., & Bandura, A. 1999. Social cognitive theory and gender development differentiation. *Psychological Review*, 106: 676–713.

Cassar, G., & H. Friedman. 2009. Does Self-efficacy Affect Entrepreneurial Investment? *Strategic Entrepreneurship Journal*, 3 (3): 241–60.

Chen, C., Greene, P., & Crick, A. 1998. Does entrepreneurial self-efficacy distinguish entrepreneurs from managers? *Journal of Business Venturing*, 13: 295–316.

Chen, G., Gully, M.S., & Eden, D. 2004. General self-efficacy and self-esteem: Toward theoretical and empirical distinction between correlated self-evaluations. *Journal of Organizational Behavior*, 25: 375–395.

Chuanyin, X. 2014. Why Do Some People Choose to Become Entrepreneurs? An Integrative Approach. *Journal Of Management Policy & Practice*, 15(1):25-38.

Contiu, L., Gabor, M., & Stefanescu, D. 2012. Hofstede's Cultural Dimensions and Student's Ability to Develop an Entrepreneurial Spirit. *Procedia - Social And Behavioral Sciences*, 46, 4th World

Conference On Educational Sciences (WCES-2012) 02-05 February 2012 Barcelona, Spain, 5553-5557.

Dibben, M., Harris, S., & Wheeler, C. 2003. Export Market Development: Planning and Relationship Processes of Entrepreneurs in Different Countries. *Journal Of International Entrepreneurship*, 1(4):383-403.

Drnovsek, M., & Glas, M. 2002. The entrepreneurial self-efficacy of nascent entrepreneurs: the case of two economies in transition. *Journal Of Enterprising Culture*, 10(2):107-131.

Evald, M., Klyver, K., & Christensen, P. 2011. The effect of human capital, social capital, and perceptual values on nascent entrepreneurs' export intentions. *Journal Of International Entrepreneurship*, 9(1):1-19.

Fayolle, A., Basso, O., & Bouchard, V. 2010. Three levels of culture and firms' entrepreneurial orientation: A research agenda. *Entrepreneurship & Regional Development*, 22(7/8):707-730.

Forlani, D. 2013. How Task Structure and Outcome Comparisons Influence Women's and Men's Risk-Taking Self-Efficacies: A Multi-Study Exploration. Psychology & Marketing, 30(12) :1088-1107.

Fourati, H., & Affes, H. 2014. Risk as a Threat, Risk as a Missing Opportunity, the Owner Finance and Entrepreneurship. *Entrepreneurship Research Journal*, 4(4): 351- 365.

Gartner, W., & Liao, J. 2012. The effects of perceptions of risk, environmental uncertainty, and growth aspirations on new venture creation success. *Small Business Economics*, 39(3): 703-712.

Geho, P., & Dangelo, J. 2012. The evolution of social media as a marketing tool for entrepreneurs. *Entrepreneurial executive*, 17:61-68.

Gist, M. E. 1989. The influence of training method on self-efficacy and idea generation among managers. *Personnel Psychology*, 42 (4): 787-805.

Hang, M., & Van Weezel, A. 2005. Media and entrepreneurship: A survey of the literature relating both concepts. *18th Scandinavian Academy of Management Meeting, Aarhus School of Business, Denmark:* 18-20.

Hayton, J., George, G., & Zahra, S. 2002. National Culture and Entrepreneurship: A Review of

Behavioral Research. *Entrepreneurship: Theory & Practice*, 26(4):33-52.

Hechavarria, D., Renko, M., & Matthews, C. 2012. The nascent entrepreneurship hub: goals, entrepreneurial self-efficacy and start-up outcomes. *Small Business Economics*, 39(3):685-701.

Hindle, K., & Klyver, K 2007. Exploring the relationship between media coverage and participation in entrepreneurship: Initial global evidence and research implications. *International Entrepreneurship & Management Journal*, 3(2):217-242.

Hopp, C., & Stephan, U. 2012. The influence of socio-cultural environments on the performance of nascent entrepreneurs: Community culture, motivation, self-efficacy and start-up success. *Entrepreneurship & Regional Development*, 24(9/10):917-945.

Kanter, R. M. 1989. *Careers and the wealth of nations: A macro-perspective on the structure and implications of career forms.* M. B. Arthur, D. T. Hall. & B. S. Lawrence (Eds.). Handbook of career theory. New York: Cambridge University Press, 506-521.

Kautonen, T., Down, S., & Minniti, M. 2014. Ageing and entrepreneurial preferences. *Small Business Economics*, 42(3):579-594.

Klyver, K., & Foley, D. 2012. Networking and culture in entrepreneurship. *Entrepreneurship & Regional Development*, 24(7/8):561-588.

Koellinger, P., M. Minniti, & C. Schade. 2006. I Think I Can, I Think I Can: Overconfidence and Entrepreneurial Behavior. *Journal of Economic Psychology*, 28:502– 527.

Kumar, R., & Kelly, L. 2006. Self-Efficacy, Social and Cultural Issues in Designing Online Technology Skills Transfer Programs: A Mexican Context. *Journal Of Information Science & Technology*, 2(4):72-92.

Lamotte, O., & Colovic, A. 2013. Do demographics influence aggregate entrepreneurship? *Applied Economics Letters*, 20(13): 1206-1210.

Lee, S.M., & Peterson, S.J. 2000. Culture, Entrepreneurial Orientation, and Global Competitiveness. *Journal of World Business*, 35(4):401-416.

Liñán, F., Fernández-Serrano, J., & Romero, I. 2013. Necessity and opportunity entrepreneurship: the mediating effect of culture, *Revista De Economía Mundial*, 33:21- 47.

Liñán, F., & Fernández-Serrano, J. 2014. National culture, entrepreneurship and economic development: different patterns across the European Union. *Small Business Economics*, 42(4):685-701.

Markatou, M., & Stournaras, Y. 2013. Innovation for entrepreneurship: is new technology a driving mechanism for the creation of a firm? *Journal Of Global Business & Technology*, 9(2):1-11.

Markman, G., Balkin, D., & Baron, R. 2002. Inventors and New Venture Formation: The Effects of General Self–Efficacy and Regretful Thinking. *Entrepreneurship: Theory & Practice*, 27(2):149-165.

McMullen, J., Shepherd, D. 2006. Entrepreneurial action and the role of uncertainty in the theory of the entrepreneur. *Academic of Management Review*, 31(1):132–152.

Méndez-Picazo, M., Galindo-Martín, M., & Ribeiro-Soriano, D. 2012. Governance, entrepreneurship and economic growth, *Entrepreneurship & Regional Development*, 24 (9/10): 865-877.

Miller, D. 2015. A Downside to the Entrepreneurial Personality? *Entrepreneurship: Theory & Practice*, January:1-8.

Montanye, J.A. 2006. Entrepreneurship. *Independent Review*, 10(4): 547-569.

Mortan, R., Ripoll, P., Carvalho, C., & Bernal, M. 2014. Effects of emotional intelligence on entrepreneurial intention and self-efficacy. *Revista De Psicología Del Trabajo Y De Las Organizaciones*, 30:97-104.

Mueller, S., & Dato-On, M. 2008. Gender-role orientation as a determinant of entrepreneurial self-efficacy. *Journal Of Developmental Entrepreneurship*, 13(1):3-20.

Navarro-García, A. 2015. Drivers of export entrepreneurship, *International business review*.

Noseleit, F. 2013. Entrepreneurship, structural change, and economic growth, *Journal Of Evolutionary Economics*, 23(4):735-766.

O'Regan, N. 2012. Entrepreneurship and innovation: Overview. *Strategic Change*, 21(5/6):193-198.

Poh Kam, W., Yuen Ping, H., & Erkko, A. 2005. Entrepreneurship, Innovation and Economic Growth: Evidence from GEM data. *Small Business Economics*, 24(3):335-350.

Reynolds, P.D., M. Hay, & S.M. Camp. 1999. *Global entrepreneurship monitor: 1999 executive report*. Kansas City: Kauffman Center.

Robinson, S., & Stubberud, H. 2014. Older and wiser? An analysis of advice networks by age, *Academy Of Entrepreneurship Journal*, 20(2): 59-70.

Rogers, E. 1995. *Diffusion of Innovations*, 4th edn. Free Press: New York, NY, 1-37.

Rozell, E., Scroggins, W., Amorós, J., Arteaga, M., & Schlemm, M. 2010. Entrepreneurship in specific cultural contexts: the role of training and development for entrepreneur-culture fit, *Journal For Global Business Education*, 10:51-71.

Sánchez, J., Carballo, T., & Gutiérrez, A. 2011. The entrepreneur from a cognitive approach. *Psicothema*, 23(3):433-438.

Schumpeter, J. 1939. *Business Cycles: A Theoretical, Historical and Statistical Analysis*. McGraw-Hill: New York, NY, 84-100.

Shane, S., 2000. Prior knowledge and the discovery of entrepreneurial opportunities. *Organization Science,* 11(4): 448-469.

Shinnar, R., Giacomin, O., & Janssen, F. 2012. Entrepreneurial Perceptions and Intentions: The Role of Gender and Culture. *Entrepreneurship: Theory & Practice*, 36(3):465-493.

Steensma, H., Marino, L., Weaver, K., & Dickson, P. 2000. The influence of national culture on the formation of technology alliances by entrepreneurial firms. *Academy Of Management Journal*, 43(5): 951-973.

Stel, A., Carree, M. & Thurik R. 2005. The Effect of Entrepreneurial Activity on National Economic Growth, *Small Business Economics*, 24:311–321.

Studdard, N., Dawson, M., & Jackson, N. 2013. Fostering Entrepreneurship and Building Entrepreneurial Self-Efficacy in Primary and Secondary Education. *Creative & Knowledge Society*, 3(2):1-15.

Swierczek, F., & Quang, T. 2004. Entrepreneurial cultures in asia: business policy or cultural imperative. *Journal Of Enterprising Culture*, 12(2) :127-145.

Umesh, U., Jessup, L., & Huynh, M. 2007. Technology entrepreneurs. *Communications of the acm*, 50(10):60-66.

Wennekers, S., Van Stel, A., Thurik, R., & Reynolds, P. 2005. Nascent entrepreneurship and the level of economic development. *Small Business Economics*, 24(3):293–309.

Williams, L., & McGuire, S. 2010. Economic creativity and innovation implementation: the entrepreneurial drivers of growth? Evidence from 63 countries. *Small Business Economics*, 4:391-412.

Wilson, F., Kickul, J., & Marlino, D. 2007. Gender, Entrepreneurial Self-Efficacy, and Entrepreneurial Career Intentions: Implications for Entrepreneurship Education. *Entrepreneurship: Theory & Practice*, 31(3):387-406.

Wilson, F., Kickul, J., Marlino, D., Barbosa, S., & Griffiths, M. 2009. An analysis of the role of gender and self-efficacy in developing female entrepreneurial interest and behavior. *Journal Of Developmental Entrepreneurship*, 14(2):105-119.

Xu, H., & Reuf, M. 2004. The myth of the risk-tolerant entrepreneur. *Strategic Organization*, 2(4):331–355.

YOUR KNOWLEDGE HAS VALUE

- We will publish your bachelor's and
  master's thesis, essays and papers

- Your own eBook and book -
  sold worldwide in all relevant shops

- Earn money with each sale

Upload your text at www.GRIN.com
and publish for free